OCEAN

HOW TINY PLANTS FEED THE SEAS

THE BLUE SKY PRESS

An Imprint of Scholastic Inc. • New York

SUNLIGHT

by **Molly Bang** &
Penny Chisholm

illustrated by **MOLLY BANG**

DIVE INTO THE SEA!
Now flip over slowly, and look up.
The water is shimmering with light—
my light.

I am your sun,
your golden star.
All ocean life depends on me;
so does all life on land.

In your forests, prairies, and
your gardens, green plants
catch my sunlight-energy.
They pump in water
from the ground

and pull in
carbon dioxide
from the air.

Plants use my energy to build these molecules into . . .

SUGAR!

All the while, the plants send oxygen into the air— the oxygen you breathe.

This is **photosynthesis:** plants making life with light—my light.

Animals—yes, animals like YOU!—eat the plants,
or you eat other animals that have eaten plants.
You are links in food chains—the chains of life.

And as you eat, you break apart the sugar from the plants

— KRAK! —

and use its energy—MY energy!—to live.
You breathe out carbon dioxide,
and the plants pull it back in.

Everything is connected.

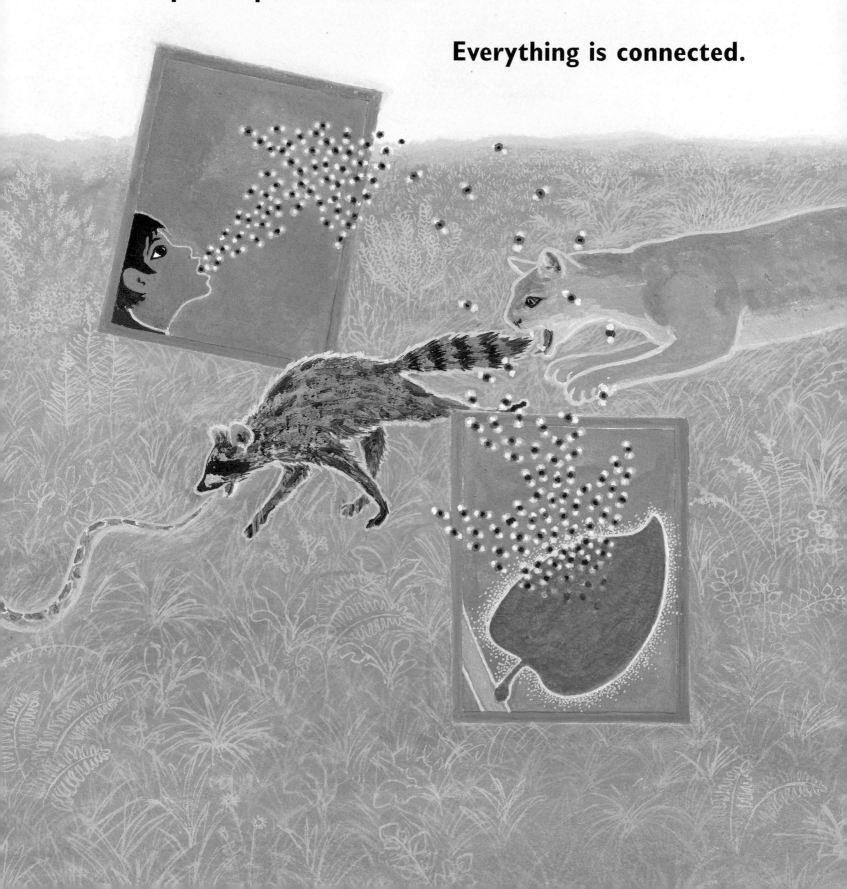

All ocean life is part
of food chains, too.
And every ocean food
chain starts when plants
catch my light.

But where
are the ocean's plants?

The seaweeds you find
growing along the shore feed
some sea creatures living THERE.

But in the vast, open ocean, far
from land, do you see seaweed forests,
seaweed gardens, seaweed prairies?

NO!
You see no green at all—none.

In the open ocean you see only

blue water.

Then where are the ocean's

green plants?

They're right before your eyes!
They're everywhere—
in countless shapes and sizes.
But they're so small you need
a microscope to see them.

A billion billion billion
of these tiny plants—that's

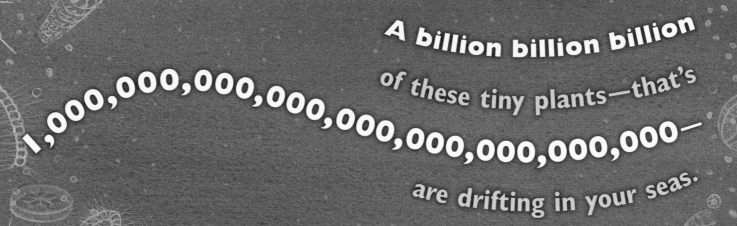

are drifting in your seas.

They are called
phytoplankton.
Phytoplankton form the great
invisible pasture of the sea.

Take a deep breath.

HALF the oxygen
you breathe every day
comes from green plants on land.

The OTHER HALF

is bubbling out of all the tiny

phytoplankton floating in your seas.

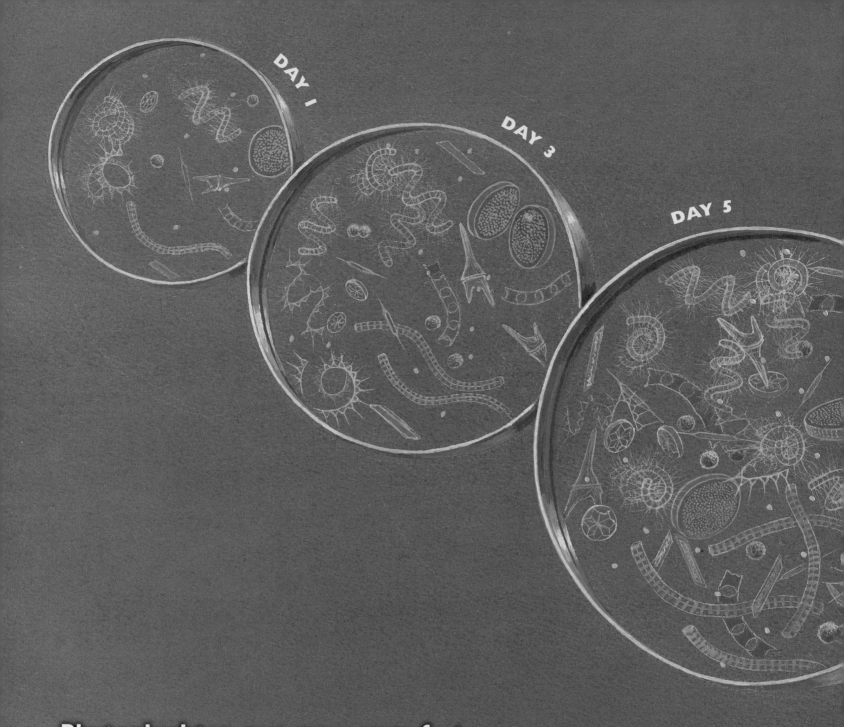

DAY 1

DAY 3

DAY 5

Phytoplankton can grow very fast.

If it has enough light and nutrients, one

phytoplankton can grow and become two

in just a day or so. It splits into identical twins!

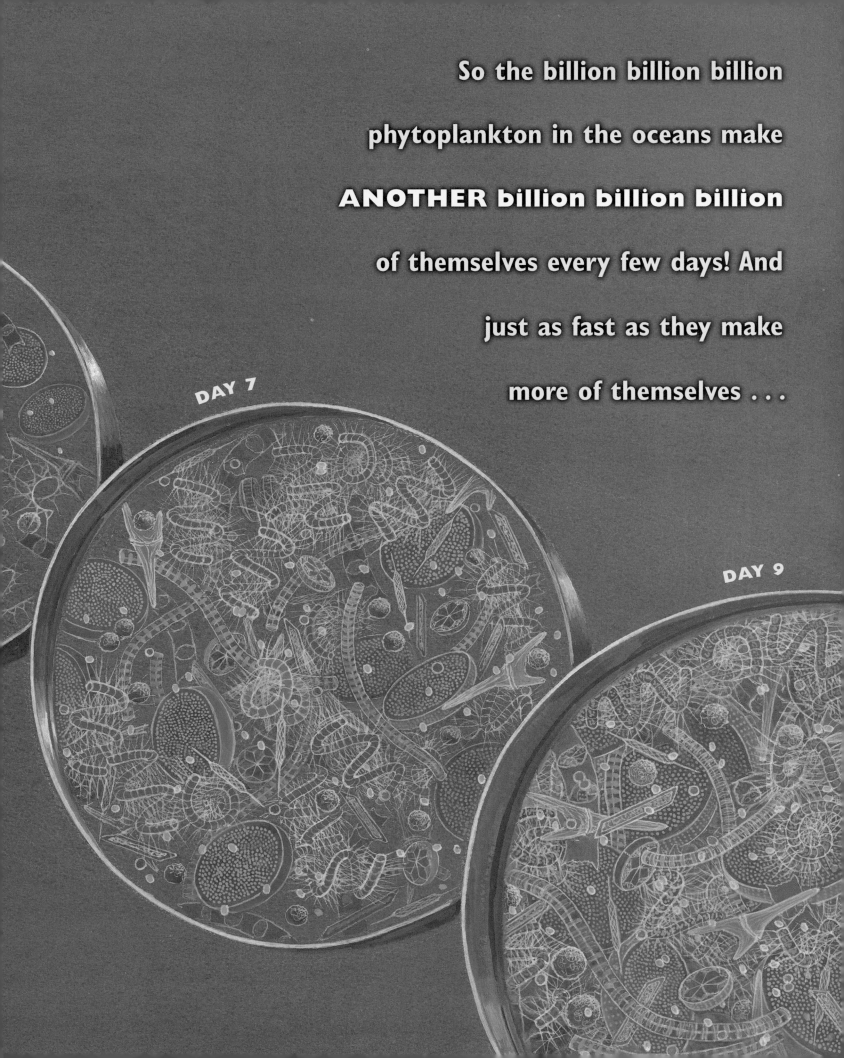

So the billion billion billion phytoplankton in the oceans make **ANOTHER** billion billion billion of themselves every few days! And just as fast as they make more of themselves . . .

DAY 7

DAY 9

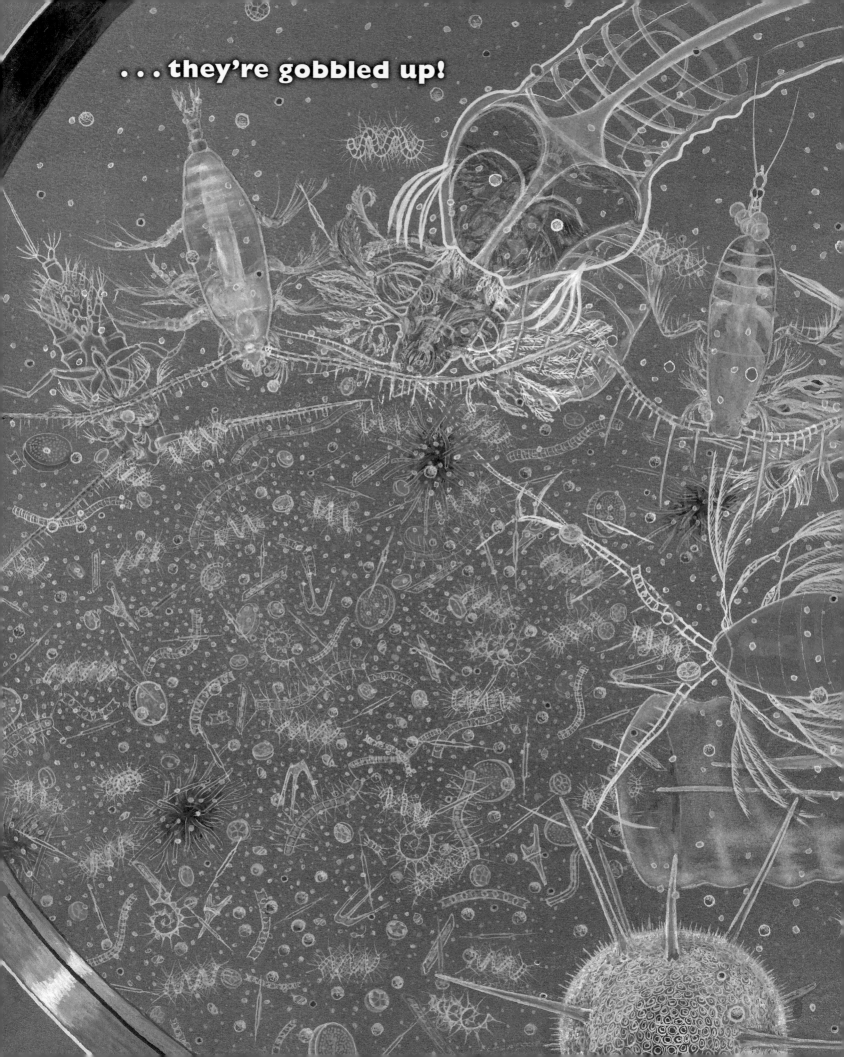

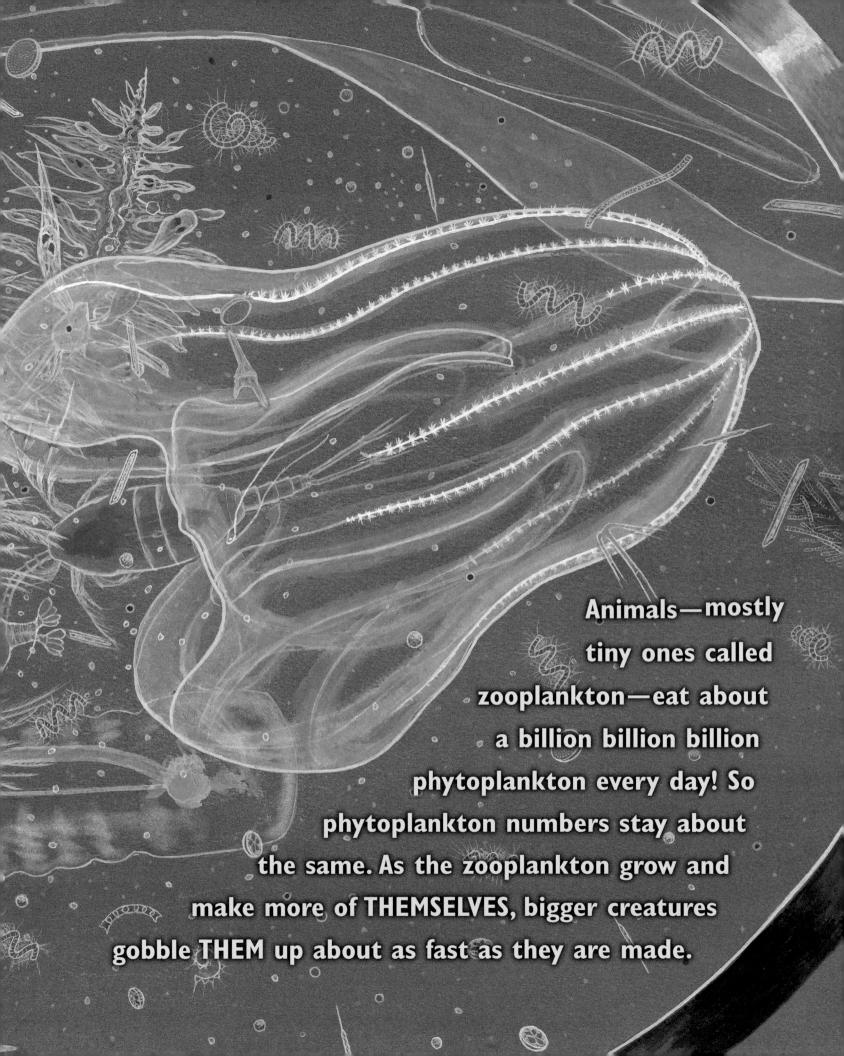

Animals—mostly tiny ones called zooplankton—eat about a billion billion billion phytoplankton every day! So phytoplankton numbers stay about the same. As the zooplankton grow and make more of THEMSELVES, bigger creatures gobble THEM up about as fast as they are made.

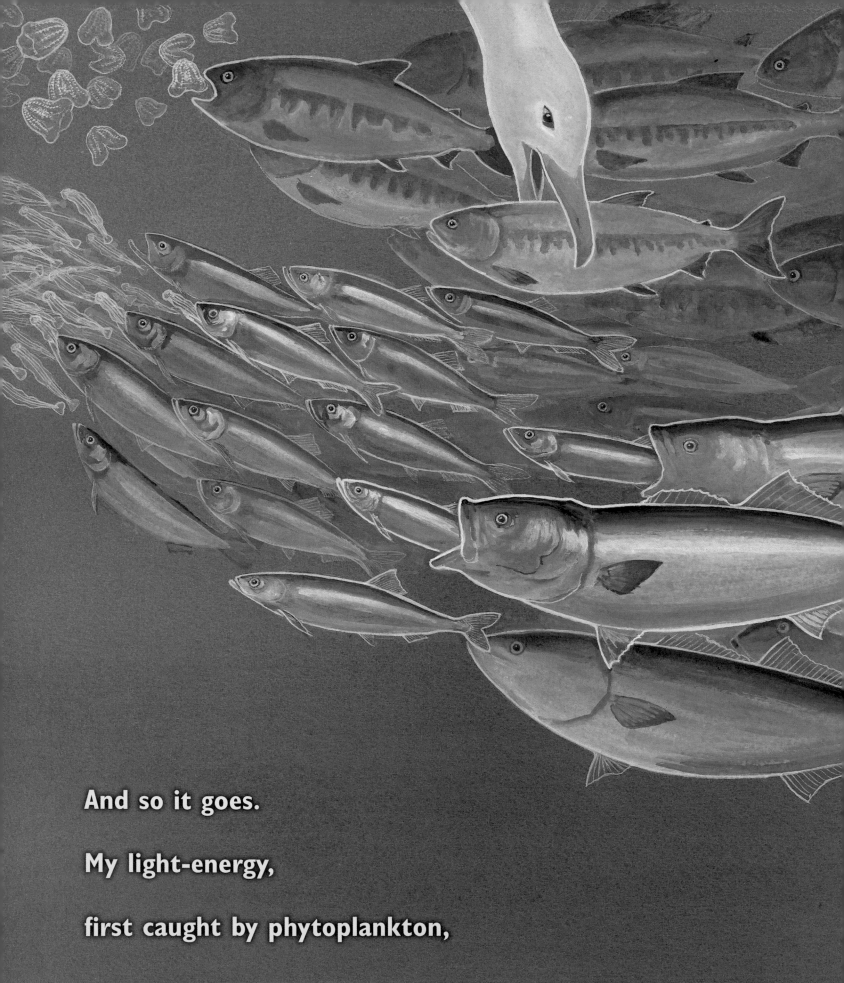

And so it goes.

My light-energy,

first caught by phytoplankton,

flows through

the ocean's chains of life,

from the tiniest green plants

to the biggest fish or whale.

But here's a puzzle for you.

My light cannot reach deeper
than the ocean's thin, top layer, so that is
where the phytoplankton have to live.

The deep cold waters underneath
are pitch black dark—darker than
the darkest, moonless, starless night.

Phytoplankton cannot live there.

But lots of animals do!

Where do *these* animals get their food?

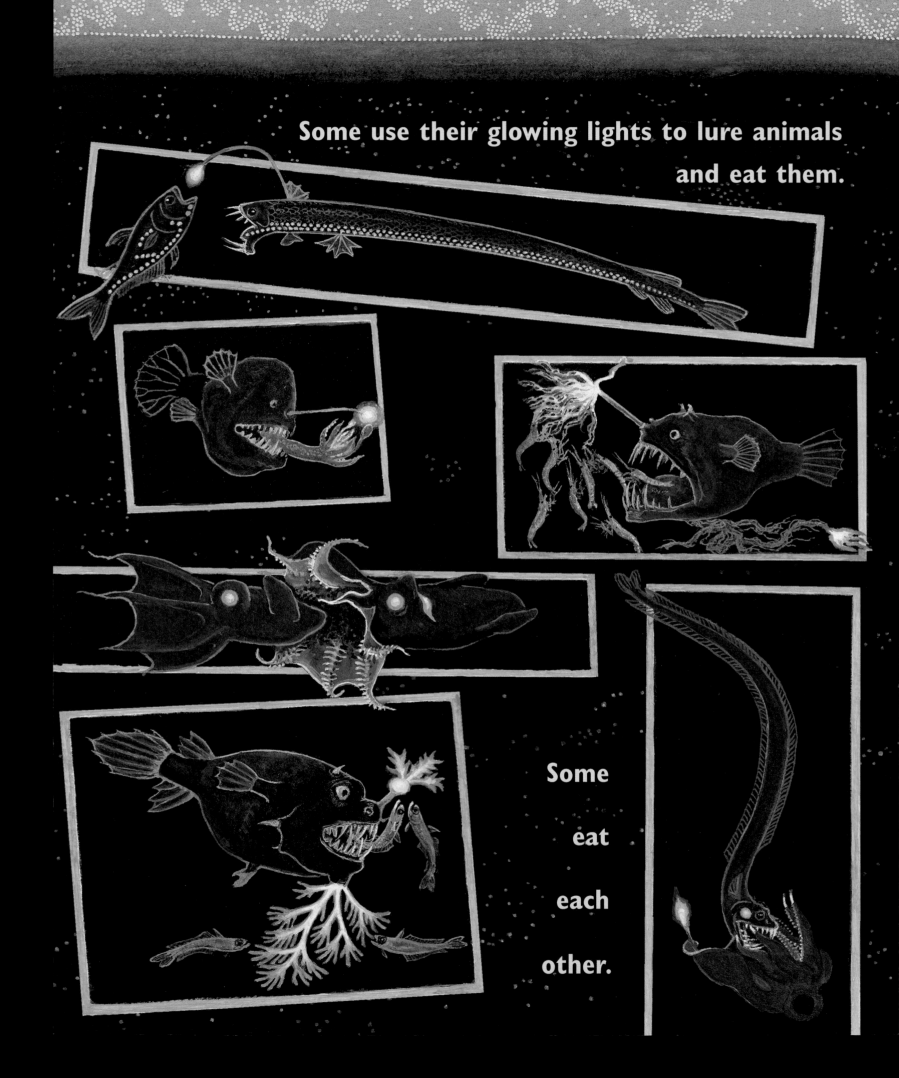

Some use their glowing lights to lure animals and eat them.

Some eat each other.

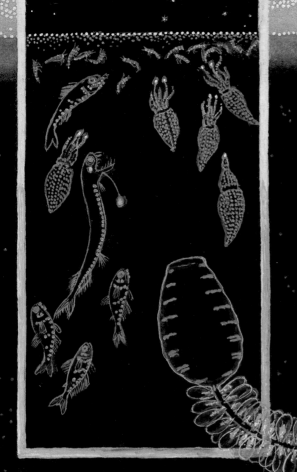

Some swim up

at night to feed

on phytoplankton.

Others wait. . . .

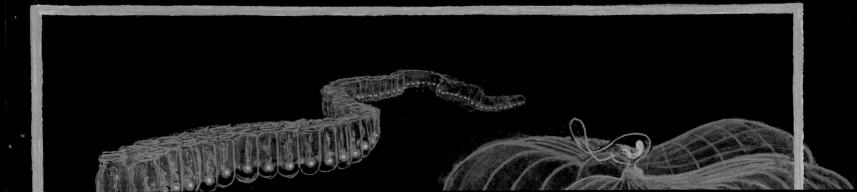

They wait for SNOW.

This snow isn't made of ice. "Marine snow" is tiny
flakes from living things. As animals and phytoplankton
live and die, their poop and mucus, carcasses and guts,
sink down and down, like falling flakes of snow.
Marine snow is nutritious food for bacteria and other
creatures living in the sunless belly of the sea.

Nothing goes to waste.

As bacteria and animals eat the falling snow,
they break it down and push
leftover nutrients and carbon dioxide
out into the black, deep sea waters.

BUT WAIT!

Phytoplankton all live in the sunlit surface waters MILES above. They need those nutrients to make more of themselves. And without more phytoplankton, the ocean animals will die!

How can those deep dark waters—rich with nutrients— rise all those miles back up into the light so the phytoplankton can use them once again?

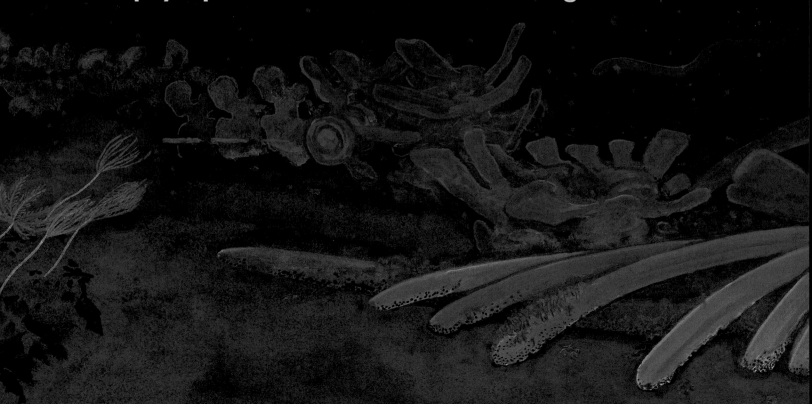

I, your sun,
pour my light
onto Earth each day.

My sunlight powers winds that build
great storms and mix the water
layers of the seas.

My light helps drive enormous currents.
They thrust the deep sea waters, rich with
nutrients and carbon dioxide, up,

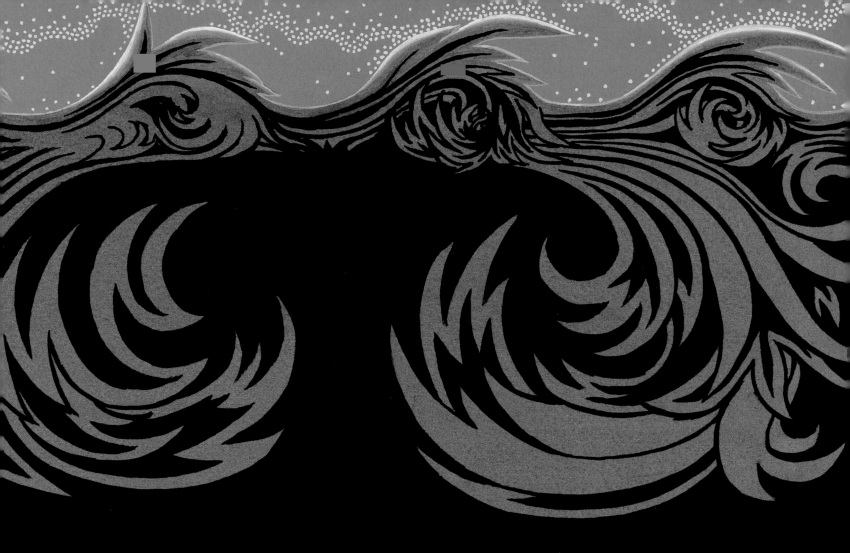

up,

up,

all the

way back

up . . .

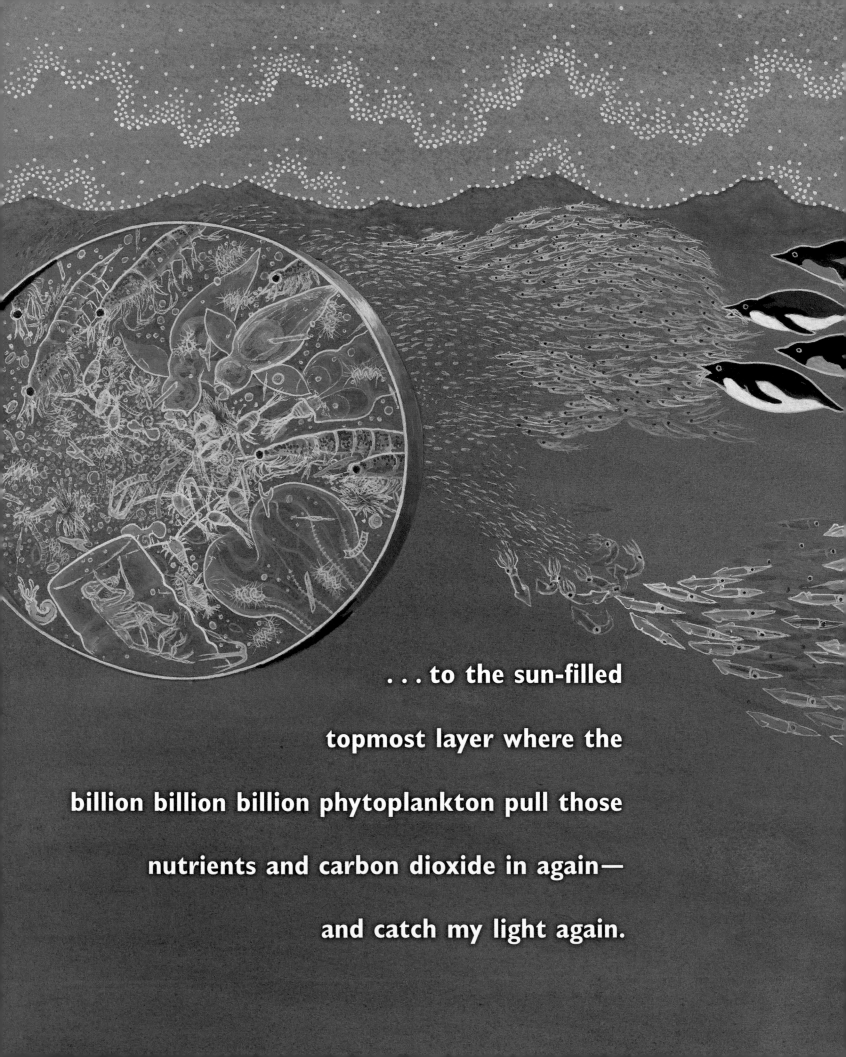

. . . to the sun-filled

topmost layer where the

billion billion billion phytoplankton pull those

nutrients and carbon dioxide in again—

and catch my light again.

Now they can keep my sunlight-energy flowing,

ever flowing,

through new chains of life.

I AM YOUR SUN.

My light gives life to your green Earth . . .

. . . and

to your deep

and restless

seas.

NOTES ABOUT THIS BOOK

The world's oceans cover seventy percent of our planet, and they teem with life. In fact, the combined weight of all the animals in the sea is roughly equal to the weight of a billion elephants! With  so many creatures living in the oceans, how do they find enough food to eat? They all depend on microscopic plants called phytoplankton that float in the sunlit topmost layer of the seas. Even life in the deepest darkest depths of the oceans depends on the growth of these sunlight-fueled plants. And—even more amazing—so do you! This "invisible pasture" produces half of the oxygen you breathe! In this book, *Ocean Sunlight*, we introduce readers to the wondrous processes taking place every moment in our seas, and we describe how most of the present forms of life on Earth—including ourselves—could not exist without them.

These notes are just a beginning; to thoroughly explain what we know about how our oceans work would require including numerous college textbooks from many fields. And with a subject so vast, there are exceptions to the generalizations we have presented. We touch on some of these below and challenge you to keep exploring!

LIFE DEPENDS ON THE SUN.

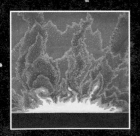

Our story begins with the sun, the golden star that lights our world. Every day, a tiny portion of the sun's heat and light strikes the Earth—but that tiny amount is much, much more than all the energy from coal, oil, and gas we use each day. (To learn more about the sun's energy, see our first book,

My Light.) Plants are able to live by catching some of this sunlight, which they use in photosynthesis, the process briefly described early in this book. (For a more detailed explanation of photosynthesis on land, see our second book, *Living Sunlight: How Plants Bring the Earth to Life*.) Fueled by the sun, photosynthesis enables plants to feed almost all living things, both on land and in the sea. It is the most important process on Earth. Without it, our planet would be a ball of rock and water—and bacteria.

PHYTOPLANKTON FEED OCEAN LIFE.

Each gallon of sunlit surface sea water is home to millions of phytoplankton. They belong to thousands of different species with varying shapes, sizes, colors, and ornamentation. Like a bountiful meadow that feeds a multitude of animals on land, these microscopic phytoplankton  create an enormous underwater "invisible pasture" that feeds all life in the sea—and produces half the oxygen in our air! Although most people have never heard of phytoplankton, these tiny plants are critically important to the existence of all life on Earth. Phytoplankton are the unsung heroes of our planet.

HOW DOES PHOTOSYNTHESIS WORK?

During photosynthesis, plants absorb sunlight using chlorophyll, a green pigment in their leaves. In this extraordinary process, plants are able to  use the sun's energy to make their own food—a form of sugar called glucose, which is "energy central" in all the functions of life. To make glucose, plants draw in carbon dioxide (CO_2) from the air and suck up water (H_2O) from the ground. They use the sun's energy to split the water into hydrogen (H) and oxygen (O_2) and link the

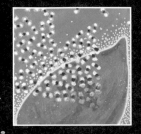

carbon atoms (C) from carbon dioxide into chains that become sugar molecules—stored energy.

Here is the chemical reaction:

CARBON DIOXIDE GAS (CO_2) + WATER (H_2O)
+ SOLAR ENERGY (PHOTONS)
react and make . . .
SUGAR ($C_6H_{12}O_6$) + OXYGEN GAS (O_2)

The illustrations in this book show oxygen atoms as white dots, carbon atoms as black dots, and hydrogen atoms as blue dots.

water
(H_2O)   carbon dioxide
(CO_2)   sugar
($C_6H_{12}O_6$)   oxygen
(O_2)

HOW DO PLANTS FEED ALL LIVING THINGS?

Through food chains. When one living thing eats another, it becomes a link in a food chain. Plants are the first link in (almost!) every food chain because they do not rely on other organisms for food. They make their own food, sugar, through

photosynthesis. Plants turn some of the sugar into proteins, fats, and other molecules that become food for the animals that eat the plants. For example, in this book you'll find an illustration where plants are eaten by mice, and the mice are eaten by a snake, which is eaten by a raccoon, which becomes food for a cougar. Each animal uses the chemical energy in its

food—energy that came originally from plants—to live and grow. Using oxygen from the air around them, animals "burn" the sugar—that is, they break apart the bonds of sugar molecules and breathe out carbon dioxide. This process is called respiration.

The chemical reaction is:

SUGAR ($C_6H_{12}O_6$) + OXYGEN GAS (O_2)
react and make . . .
CARBON DIOXIDE GAS (CO_2)
+ WATER (H_2O) + CHEMICAL ENERGY

The carbon dioxide released in respiration becomes available for plants to use again in photosynthesis.

Each year on Earth, billions of tons of plant

material are produced through photosynthesis. Much of this plant material is consumed by animals and respired back into the atmosphere as CO_2 while oxygen is consumed. Carbon and oxygen keep cycling between the plants and animals, driven by the flow of the sun's energy.

WHAT FEEDS THE FOOD CHAINS OF THE SEA?

Photosynthesis, of course! The sun provides ocean plants with the energy they need to grow and reproduce, exactly as it does for plants on land. But the majority of the ocean's photosynthesis is done by phytoplankton.

Some phytoplankton facts:

• You need a microscope to see all but the largest phytoplankton.

• The thousands of different species have a size range far greater than we can show in these illustrations.

Members of the smallest

species are 1/100th the width of a human hair. If the smallest phytoplankton were the size of a pea, the largest would be the size of a hot air balloon!

- Phytoplankton are some- 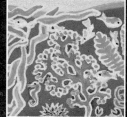 times called "algae." Many are distantly related to the seaweeds lining our seashores.
- Phytoplankton are responsible for half the photosynthesis on Earth, even though their collective weight is only 0.1% of all plants and trees on land.
- Finally, while this book focuses on ocean phytoplankton, they have close cousins who live in in our ponds, marshes, streams, soils, and even in ice! Where there is water and sunlight, you will usually find phytoplankton.

HOW PHOTOSYNTHESIS CHANGED EARTH'S ATMOSPHERE

Three billion years ago, when primitive ocean bacteria were the only life on Earth, there was no oxygen in Earth's atmosphere! But some of

 those primitive bacteria were the ancestors of the phytoplankton we see today, and they developed the ability to photosynthesize. As they spread and evolved and grew and photosynthesized over more than a billion years, the oxygen they released slowly leaked into the atmosphere. Had this not happened, the plentiful oxygen we all breathe today would not exist!

HOW CAN SUCH TINY ORGANISMS PRODUCE SO MUCH?

Phytoplankton are streamlined "photosynthesis machines." Since they have no stems or trunks or roots to maintain, they use all of the products of

their photosynthesis to grow and multiply. When they have enough sunlight and all the nutrients they need—such as the nitrogen, phosphorus, and iron that all living things require for their metabolism— phytoplankton can double their numbers each day. At this rate, a single phytoplankton cell could grow into a billion cells in just one month! Sometimes phytoplankton "bloom" this way in shallow ponds, marshes, and coastal waters that are rich with nutrients that have flowed in from the land—largely from fertilizers and untreated sewage. When this happens, the phytoplankton grow faster than they can

 be eaten and form dense patches that slowly sink to the bottom. Bacteria feast on these patches, and as they do, they respire and consume so much oxygen— more than the phytoplank- ton can produce—that the fish and other sea life cannot live there anymore. This is what causes the "dead zones" in some coastal waters; their ecosystems have become unbalanced because the influx of nutrients from the land has caused phytoplankton population explosions.

WHAT ABOUT OCEAN AREAS FAR FROM LAND?

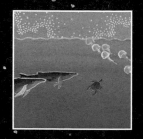

In the vast open oceans, away from land, there is still abundant sunlight and CO_2 for photosynthesis, but nutrients are scarce; they are available only through recycling from within the ocean system, and this limits the growth of phyto- plankton. If you build a house, for example, you may have plenty of carpenters and lumber, but the size of your house and how fast you can build it will depend on your supply of nails—which are small but essential. Similarly, phytoplankton growth and reproduction depends on the supply of nutrients available.

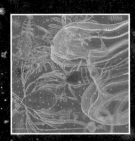

And since phytoplankton are generally eaten as fast as they reproduce, their population stays about the same. It may be difficult to imagine how something that is constantly changing— growing and dying—appears to stay the same. Imagine a bathtub half filled with water. Now open the drain and turn on the faucet so the flow in equals the flow out. The amount of water in the tub stays the same, but the water going down the drain is replaced by new water. In a similar way, phytoplankton are constantly reproducing, replacing those that are being eaten or dying, so their numbers stay about the same—just as the amount of water in the tub stays the same. It is only when the flow in and the flow out are not equal—when the growth and death are not the same—that the balance is disrupted. This concept is very important, and applies to all living things in a food chain.

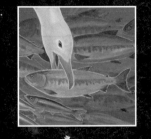

HOW DOES THE FOOD CREATED BY PHYTOPLANKTON REACH LIFE IN THE DEEP OCEAN?

Because both water and phytoplankton absorb sunlight, the oceans get darker and darker the deeper down you go. Below six hundred feet (the length of two football fields) there is no light—none—and, with no light, there are no phytoplankton. If the

ocean were a twenty-story building, there would be light and phytoplankton only on the top story. The surface waters are like a thin, green, living film that feeds all life in the sea.

But nature has lots of ways to distribute its bounty! During the day, many animals spend their time hovering below the sunlit surface layers and then swim up at night to eat phytoplankton. This way, they're protected from predators by darkness. Just before dawn, they swim back down to the safety of the dark, deep waters.

Many other animals spend their entire lives in the deep sea. Some feed on each other, often luring their prey with appendages that glow with blue light. Others feed on "marine snow."

WHAT EXACTLY IS MARINE SNOW?

Marine snow is tiny bits of organic matter— matter made by living things—that have been sloughed off of creatures as they are eaten or as they die and fall apart. Each "snowflake" is

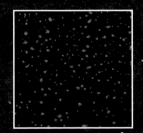

colonized by microbes that live off its nutrients, turning it into a tiny oasis of life. As each piece of snow settles slowly down and down, the microbes digest it and grow. They, too, become food for the deep sea animals. Very little reaches the bottom of the sea.

Some deep sea organisms have elaborate devices for capturing marine snowflakes,

which are their source of food. What looks like a big creature in this illustration, for example, is actually a three- to six-foot-wide net of mucus made by the tiny, inch-long larvacean that's inside! The larvacean uses the net to catch the falling "snow."

IS MARINE SNOW THE ONLY FOOD THE BOTTOM DWELLERS EAT?

No. Every once in a while a dead whale (or other large animal) sinks to the bottom—a "whale fall." Whole ecosystems immediately assemble to feast. It takes decades for the whale to be completely consumed, bones and all. The little feathery red worms on the bones in the illustration

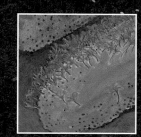

are Osedax ("bone devourers"), the last guests at the banquet. Ultimately, everything is eaten.

Remember, each bit of organic matter that settles to the deep sea can be traced back to sugar formed by the photosynthesis of phytoplankton in the surface waters. As this matter is consumed by animals and bacteria of the deep, it is converted back into CO_2, which, along with nutrients, is excreted into the deep sea water and trapped in the deep ocean.

TRAPPED? WHY?

The physics of the oceans are complex (the subject of another book!) and intimately connected with all that lives there. The top few

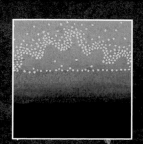

hundred feet of ocean waters are diluted by rain and kept relatively warm by the sun. These surface waters remain above the colder, saltier, and thus heavier, waters below,

and the two layers do not mix easily. When marine snow settles from the surface and decomposes in the deep water, the nutrients and carbon dioxide that have been released tend to stay there. But not forever.

TO KEEP THE OCEAN ALIVE, WHAT GOES DOWN MUST COME UP.

Deep waters, and the nutrients and carbon dioxide they carry, have several ways to return to the surface. First, when surface waters cool in winter, winds are strong enough to mix the water downward and force some deep water up. Second, along the western coasts of continents, winds blow surface waters offshore, and deep water rises to replace them. Finally, the oceans are connected through global ocean circulation—a sort of "conveyer belt"—propelled by a variety of forces, including the sun's energy. Over vast regions, the belt sends very deep water up to the surface layer, replenishing the supply of nutrients that the phytoplankton need to keep thriving.

If you were able to ride on this conveyer belt, it would take you about fifteen hundred years to complete the journey through all the oceans, moving between the surface and deep waters. All the oceans of our planet are connected in this way.

ADDITIONAL INFORMATION

There are so many important, related concepts that we could not possibly cover them all in this book.

For simplicity, we say, "all life in the oceans depends on phytoplankton photosynthesis." This is not completely true. "Chemosynthetic" bacteria, for example, can use the energy contained in chemical compounds to turn carbon dioxide into sugar without the sun. We do not yet know how abundant they are in the sea. We do know they form the base of the food chains around the deep sea volcanoes—the hydrothermal vents that exist in various places on the ocean floor. The bright red tubeworms in

one of the illustrations are filled with chemosynthetic bacteria. These are symbiotic bacteria—they use the worms as their home and feed them in return.

In our discussion, we have also shortchanged massive amounts of bacteria that float everywhere in the sea and are central to "ocean metabolism." These are not the kinds of bacteria that cause human disease, which are only a tiny, tiny fraction of Earth's bacteria. On the contrary, these are among the huge majority of bacteria that maintain our planet.

A million of these ocean bacteria live in every teaspoon of sea water. Many of them grow by using the carbon compounds made by phyto-plankton during photosynthesis. Others, as we do discuss in the book, grow on particles like marine snow. In the process, they release nitrogen, phosphorus, iron, and other nutrients— recycling them for use by other living things. These bacteria are also vital to the ocean's food chains.

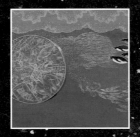

WHY SHOULD WE CARE SO MUCH ABOUT UNDERSTANDING OUR OCEANS?

Because our lives depend on them. As land-dwellers, we tend to think of oceans as alien worlds—vast and limitless—relatively immune to our influence. Yet in the past few hundred years, we have begun to change the chemistry of ocean waters and life in the sea. We did not discuss

these issues in *Ocean Sunlight* because our intent was to describe how ocean life works, not to sound alarms. Through understanding ocean ecosystems, we can make better decisions about how to live on this remarkable planet that keeps us alive. We hope this book encourages you to learn more!

To my Green Sustenance
and to Monika, my Other Sustenance — M.B.

To all my students, *Prochlorococcus*, and Don, who have taught me much — P.C.

With MANY thanks, especially to Jim Green! And to Bruce Robison, Larry Madin, Steve Rintoul, John Cullen, Tom Malone, Trish and Dave Munro, Nadav Kashtan, Jessie Thompson, Katya Frois-Moniz, and to the whole Lasche family. And to Kathy Westray, Grace Kendall, and Carol & Bonnie Verburg, and finally to Elaine Markson, who got it through!

THE BLUE SKY PRESS

Text copyright © 2012 by Molly Bang and Penny Chisholm
Illustrations copyright © 2012 by Molly Bang
All rights reserved.
No part of this publication may be reproduced, stored in a retrieval system, or transmitted in any form or by any means, electronic, mechanical, photocopying, recording, or otherwise, without written permission of the publisher.
For information regarding permission, please write to: Permissions Department, Scholastic Inc., 557 Broadway, New York, New York 10012.
SCHOLASTIC, THE BLUE SKY PRESS, and associated logos are trademarks and/or registered trademarks of Scholastic Inc.
Library of Congress catalog card number: 2011024823
ISBN 978-0-545-27322-0
10 9 8 7 6 5 4 3 2 1   12 13 14 15 16
Printed in Singapore 46

This book was printed on paper containing 55% recycled content and 25% post-consumer waste.
First printing, May 2012
Designed by Kathleen Westray

DATE DUE

GAYLORD			PRINTED IN U.S.A.